Tales fro
Over The Moon
Molly Mop & Bucket

Would you like a free e-book?

Busy Miss Hoover

(first in the series)

is now available for FREE on amazon.com

bookstore and Apple iBooks.

Harold's Tale from Over the Moon

(second in the series)

Is now available

on Amazon and Apple Books.

If you would like to receive all our latest publishing news, newfound treasures and information on the next publication, do sign up for the newsletter.

You will find the newsletter on our website

www.ireadyouread.com

CassGriffin Publishing
61 Bridge Street
Kingston
HR5 3DJ
United Kingdom
Author : Pauline Dawber
Illustrator : Ricky Audi

Published 2023

ISBN 9781513665658

iRead youRead

ireadyouread.com

To my Ballet Master

The Late Mr. Andrew Hardie

Tales from

Over The Moon

Molly Mop & Bucket

.......STICKPLAYERS EXTRAORDINAIRE

Author : Pauline Dawber

Illustrator : Ricky Audi

Reggie Lemon's Hardware Store is a
treasure trove of all things useful.
Things that are meant for the
everyday running of a household.

Screws, nuts, bolts, iron garden gates,
garden implements, washers, wing nuts,
all the power tools you could possibly want,
brushes, bins, hinges, chains, wicker baskets,
birdseed and of course, mops and buckets.

Surprisingly, and many agree
that all these tools are beautiful.
They are good to look at and good to handle.

REGGIE LEMON HARDWARE

Reggie Lemon is a tall, handsome and wonderfully talented carpenter. He usually wears his trilby hat and braces, and always polishes his shoes. He makes every moment count, loves his store and knows where everything is kept.

"Could I just have two grub screws? Reggie?"
"Of course!"

And he quickly puts the two screws from the draw into a brown paper bag.
"6p please!"

Molly Mop and Bucket first met in
Reggie Lemon's Hardware store.

Somehow, they always make sure that
they are never sold separately.

At 5:00 o'clock every evening,
the door lock is turned shut.

Reggie Lemon has finished
his working day and goes home for tea.

REGGIE LEMON HARDWARE

The world seems quiet and
dark inside the store.
The cool night air steps in, silently.

There are a few whispers of sounds:
clocks ticking, metal implements
pinging and soft cracking noises
as the temperature drops.

Most of the screws, nails and things
like bird seed continue to sleep on
into the dark of the night.

But the cold night air is not sleepy.
The cold night air is wide awake and crispy.

Bird Seed

Old Sparky, the metal electric fire on display, makes a loud pinging noise and a funny thing happens. He flips into the middle of the floor, switches himself on and starts telling everyone about amps, volts, frequencies... all things electricity!

And even, how at 21 degrees centigrade, the air around us is full of molecules, whizzing at an incredible 1000 miles per hour!

Getting hotter and hotter and hotter and hotter, Old Sparky is going for the 21 degrees centigrade. He simply becomes more heated and excited.

Luckily, Old Sparky has the controls. No Fire Fighters are needed this time.

Of course, he is talking to a mainly sleeping audience, but he doesn't care. Most nights he likes to talk about the wonders of electricity and the air around us.

The next morning, you would never have guessed that the cold night air had changed a few small things. That same morning, Busy Miss Hoover comes to the store. She needs a new mop and bucket to replace her old ones.

Reggie Lemon is happy to oblige.

And so it is that Molly Mop and Bucket come to enjoy the life they are leading with Busy Miss Hoover and her friends.

Molly Mop and Bucket have also made the long, frankly uncomfortable journey, across the Mountains of the Moon to join their friends and live on Over The Moon.

On Over The Moon, the Man in the Moon can only be seen on a Saturday afternoon. Molly Mop and Bucket meet up with him.

Up close, the Man in the Moon smells rather cheesy and Bucket wants to throw cold water all over him and Molly Mop wants to wash him down with beautiful smelling Italian soap. But, they are far too polite to do anything of the sort.

There is something yummy, though, about the Man in the Moon.

Molly Mop and Bucket didn't really know whether they should be thinking like that about a cheesy smelling Man in the Moon.

But somehow... he is quite charming!

Everyone living on Over The Moon owns a thinking hat. It is just what they all do. Usually, everybody's thinking hat really, really suits them. Thinking hats helps them to think more clearly.
You simply pop one on your head......
and "aha!" what to do next,
for the best, is easy.

Whether you are walking, sitting, standing and for however long, wearing your thinking hat is wonderful.

Yes, daydreaming about yourself
and what makes you feel happy and
well is another very important
part of wearing your thinking hat.

"I'm going shopping for my new thinking hat" says Molly Mop to Bucket.

Bucket takes an enormous saucepan and places it on his head......
"What do you think, Molly M.?"

"I'll rattle your saucepan! says Molly Mop.
"Come with me and we can both agree on our choice of hats."

With no more messing about, no hesitating or wondering whether a particular hat was better than the other.....

Molly Mop chooses a beret and Bucket chooses a safari hat.

The evenings on Over The Moon are spent telling stories around the fire-pit and catching up with the adventures of the day. Had you met a total stranger? or did you see the Cat that Sat on the Mat or had you seen Arthur, whose car is a Jaguar, which he drives far too fast.

The Man in the Moon had been a total stranger to Molly Mop and Bucket. When they met, it was October and as The Man in the Moon had explained, he was meeting up with six planets that month.......

Saturn, Venus, Jupiter, Mars, Mercury, and Uranus. "That's awesome" Molly Mop and Bucket chimed together.

This evening, it is Molly Mop and Bucket's turn to tell a story around the fire-pit.....
They both hail from Moplandvia.

So they tell the story of Queen Spongia and King Aqua of Moplandvia.
To begin with ....

Molly Mop and Bucket present their friends with a long broomstick each.
(without the brush on the end)
They continue..........

and show their friends a map of the World.
Somewhere is Moplandvia.

The World and Moplandvia

Queen Spongia and King Aqua rule Moplandvia with an iron rod........
Well, sort of, kind of, more exactly and precisely with something they call StickPlay.

Any evil or wicked doings, the punishment is "do some more StickPlay."

Any brilliant inventions or kindnesses, the reward is "just practise your StickPlay."

Spongia and Aqua have whole stores of different kinds of sticks.
Chopsticks, fiddlesticks, candlesticks, dip sticks, matchsticks, walking sticks, swordsticks, bread sticks, broomsticks, pick up sticks, lipsticks drumsticks
and many more............

StickPlay is a skilful art.
And twizzling the sticks is the best part.
"We are now going to show you twizzling Stick Play....and then we are going to teach you all how to do it." Molly Mop and Bucket are masters at twizzling.

Everyone steps back.

Like windmills caught in a gale, whistling, whirring, blurring, cracking sounds quickly filled the air. Strong arms, strong shoulders and steady feet are 'must haves'. The twizzling gets faster and faster and faster.

'Impressive'... thinks everyone!

"Be bold with your sticks " shouts Molly Mop. "Bless me!" thinks Busy Miss Hoover as the sweat pours down her face.

The Fiddler, also overflowing with sweat, thwacked his stick on the ground and paused for a moment to say....
'Actually, I would stop all my plans, I would talk all day about it, I would go to bed late, and I would practise everyday, just because I want to learn StickPlay"

Harold, as much as he loves talking, is silent.

The Birds, Kassuku, Inflatable and Tumbleweed have long decided to use their sticks as perches. StickPlay just isn't for them.

That leaves Busy Miss Hoover, The Fiddler, Molly Mop and Bucket and Harold to practise the twizzling.

It is not a long and lazy night
for the students of StickPlay.
They train seriously but have
so much fun together.
The more they practice the more they begin
to know what it is to have the swiftness, and
the power of StickPlay.

Their giggles fly through the stars.
The Mountains of the Moon catch their
twizzling laughter, package it and bounce it
back to them,

again and again!
Sitting on the edge of their perches,
Kassuku, Inflatable and Tumbleweed watch
their friends become very
lively as they practise.

As the dawn says goodbye to the night, the
Birds sing their favourite songs to the
feisty, daring but happy Stick Players!

THE END

iRead youRead

ireadyouread.com

I hope you enjoy reading Molly
Mop and Bucket's short story.
This is the 3rd in a series of 6
Tales from Over The Moon

Please visit our website
www.ireadyouread.com

Sign up for the newsletter, grab yourself a free
e-book, and catch up with the latest publications!
Busy Miss Hoover is now available for FREE
On amazon.com bookstore and Apple iBooks

Happy Reading
Pauline

iRead youRead

ireadyouread.com

About The Author

My writing came about organically, it wasn't something I had planned, as it were.

I have always loved reading and books have been an amazing support for me throughout my life. They have travelled everywhere with me.

As a youngster, my family lived overseas. My Grandmother used to send (from the UK) rolled up comics every week to my sister and I.

At the time we lived in Kuala Lumpur, Malaysia. The comics were one of the highlights of the week

.

To this day, Dennis the Menace, Desperate Dan, and Beryl the Peril, remain on the list of my best loved characters!

OVER THE MOON

Printed in Great Britain
by Amazon

46592172R00025